Title: Jesus Was Funnier Than You Think
Subtitle: Discovering the Wit and Joy of Jesus in the Gospels
Written by: Christian A. Dickinson

Illustrations by: Learning Engineered LLC
Published by: Learning Engineered Publishing

Library of Congress Control Number: 2025935044
ISBN (Print): 978-1-965741-51-1

First Edition: 2025

Printed & Created in: United States of America
Text and Illustration Copyright © 2025

Learning Engineered Publishing is a division of Learning Engineered LLC and a subsidiary of Carpe Diem Unlimited Holdings, Inc.

LEARNING ENGINEERED
PUBLISHING

Contents

Dedication

To my former teacher, FCA Sponsor, and Coach turned lawyer—**Michael J. Duggar, Esquire.**

The most sarcastic, cynical, satirist, and argumentative Christian I know.
Thank you for sharpening my mind, challenging my beliefs, and proving that faith and wit make an unstoppable combination.

Also, thank you for the endless theological debates—especially the ones where you tried to convince me that free will is an illusion and that I was *predestined* to lose the argument.

— With appreciation and a begrudging nod to your endless Calvinist logic.

Introduction

Picture a Galilean hillside at dusk. A small fire crackles. Jesus sits among His disciples, the crowd murmuring nearby. He leans forward, eyes bright, and says:

"Picture a man with a plank sticking out of his eye, squinting to pluck a speck from his friend's. What a sight!"

Laughter ripples through the group—Peter snorts, John elbows Andrew, even the crowd chuckles at the absurd image. This isn't just a lesson about hypocrisy; it's a moment of joy—a glimpse of a Savior who teaches with a grin. That's the Jesus I want you to meet.

I grew up in a home buzzing with missionary families, the Gospels read aloud nightly at a creaky wooden table. Yet the Jesus I pictured was solemn, as if holiness demanded a furrowed brow. Laughter felt out of place. Even so, I sensed a spark in those stories—a warmth that drew children to Him and kept rough-edged disciples close. Over time, that spark faded under sober lessons.

Then came *The Chosen*. On screen I met a Jesus who teased His friends, laughed over meals, and used humor like a master storyteller. It wasn't irreverent—it was magnetic. Those childhood glimpses of a joyful Jesus rushed back, and I realized this wasn't a modern invention. The Gospels had shown it all along. Later, my friend Nick V. handed me *Ante Pacem*, a study of early Christian art: in the catacombs, Jesus smiles. The early church knew a Savior who was both the Man of Sorrows and the Messiah of joy. Somewhere along the way, we misplaced His grin.

This book is an invitation to find it again.

I'm not a theologian; I'm a mathematician who loves patterns. And in the Gospels I see a pattern that changes everything: Jesus taught with humor—not cheap gags, but purposeful wit that disarmed doubters, softened hard truths, and bonded followers. He painted absurd pictures (camels through needle's eyes), teased to stretch faith (calling James and John "Sons of Thunder"), told satirical parables that flipped assumptions, and dropped razor-edged lines that left experts speechless. His humor exposed hypocrisy, sparked growth, and revealed a joy so compelling that children ran to Him and crowds stayed.

We'll walk through that joy together. Each chapter blends story, Scripture, and cultural insight, with reflection questions for personal or group use. You can read straight through or jump to what grabs you. Scan the QR code for a 6-week Bible study with passages and action steps.

My challenge: reread the Gospels picturing Jesus with a grin. Let His joy ignite yours.

Chapter 1

Unpacking the Laughing Messiah

A Campfire and a Punchline

I magine a dusty Galilean evening. The air is warm with cedar smoke and the tang of sea salt from the lake. Jesus sits by a crackling campfire, His disciples sprawled on the ground, sandals caked with dust. The crowd lingers, weary but captivated, as sparks leap into the starry sky.

Jesus leans forward, His eyes glinting with mischief, and says:

"Picture a man with a massive plank jutting out of his eye, stumbling around, trying to pick a speck out of his friend's. What a sight!"

Peter snorts, nearly choking on bread. Matthew chuckles, likely picturing a smug Pharisee. The crowd bursts into laughter. And then—silence. Because beneath the comedy is a cutting truth: hypocrisy is absurd, and Jesus exposes it with a grin.

We often read Matthew 7:3–5 as a stern warning. But what if it was also a punchline? What if Jesus—the greatest teacher who ever lived—used laughter as a razor-sharp tool to make truth unforgettable? His humor wasn't comic relief. It was divine pedagogy, truth taught through a grin.

A Savior Who Smiles

We picture Jesus preaching on hillsides, healing the broken, or weeping in Gethsemane—and He did all that. But being fully human also meant laughter and joy. Children swarmed Him (Matthew 19:14). Children don't run toward dour, joyless adults. His disciples—fishermen, a tax collector, a zealot—followed Him for three years through dusty roads and stormy seas. No way that crew didn't share belly laughs over late-night fires or playful jabs along the way.

Imagine Jesus ribbing Peter about his big mouth, or teasing Thomas for always needing proof. Those moments weren't trivial. They were glue—the humor of friendship that bound them together.

The early church understood this. In the catacombs, Christians painted Jesus smiling. Scholar Graydon Snyder notes that these frescoes captured Him not only as the *Man of Sorrows* (Isaiah 53:3) but also as the One who promised, *"My joy may be in you...and your joy may be complete"* (John 15:11). Over time, solemn portraits buried that grin. But the Gospels never lost it. Jesus carried the cross, yes—but He also carried joy.

Humor With a Holy Purpose

Jesus didn't tell jokes for cheap laughs. His humor had a mission:

- Exposing hypocrisy with wit the

self-righteous couldn't dodge.

- Nudging disciples with playful banter that sparked growth.

- Engaging doubters with clever wordplay that cracked open closed hearts.

- Making truth unforgettable—because who forgets a camel squeezing through a needle's eye?

Take the plank-in-the-eye quip. In Greek, *dokos* means a load-bearing beam, not a twig. Picture someone blundering through a marketplace, a timber jutting from their eye, offering to perform delicate eye surgery on a friend. Ridiculous? Exactly. First-century Jews would've roared at the image, while Pharisees shifted uneasily. Jesus' humor wasn't cruel—it was a mirror with a grin.

Or consider another zinger: *"You strain out a gnat but swallow a camel!"* (Matthew 23:24). The crowd laughed. Gnats were the tiniest unclean pests; camels the largest unclean animals in Israel. Imagine a Pharisee carefully filtering his wine, then gulping down a camel—humps and all. The absurdity made their hypocrisy unforgettable.

The Jewish Art of Laughter

Jesus' humor was cultural as well as divine. Jewish teachers often used exaggeration, absurd scenarios, and irony to wake up their listeners. Wild word pictures weren't random—they were expected. Jesus simply perfected the art.

Think about it: when was the last time you forgot a funny story? Humor lodges truth in the heart. That's why teachers today sprinkle in jokes, and why parents use playful exaggeration with their kids. Jesus knew this. He painted outrageous images not to entertain, but to make eternal truth stick.

Why Humor Hits Home

Modern research now confirms what Jesus modeled: laughter disarms hostility, bonds communities, and helps truth endure. It lowers stress, boosts memory, and builds trust. The same principles that help teachers connect with students or parents with children are woven into the way Jesus taught.

Picture Him at your church picnic today, smiling as He says:
"Careful pointing out that burnt burger—check the plank in your eye first!"

Not mocking. Not shallow. Just memorable, transforming truth delivered with a grin.

Holiness Meets Hilarity

We've often treated holiness and humor like opposites. But Jesus reveals them as partners. He was not only the *Man of Sorrows*. He was also the Messiah of joy, wielding humor like a sculptor's chisel to shape hearts.

His laughter wasn't distraction—it was revelation. It reflected the God who *"sits in the heavens and laughs"* (Psalm 2:4). Imagine Him at your Bible study, grinning as He teases:

"Still sweating the small stuff? Try loving like I do—it's funnier."

His humor invites us to rethink faith—not as grim duty, but as a joyful adventure. Holiness doesn't silence laughter. It deepens it.

Reflection Questions

Spot the Plank
Where are you quick to notice "specks" in others while ignoring your own "planks"? How might Jesus' humor invite you to face this with humility and a smile?

The Power of Laughter
Think of a time when humor helped you hear or accept a hard truth. How could Jesus' wit do the same in your spiritual life?

Picturing Jesus' Joy
When you imagine Jesus laughing by a campfire, how does it change the way you approach Him in prayer or worship?

Try a Little Humor

This week, how can you use gentle, Jesus-style humor to encourage someone or make truth stick?

Chapter 2

Walking with the Messiah—and Getting Teased

A Storm and a Smile

Picture a stormy night on the Sea of Galilee. Waves crash against a creaky wooden boat, the disciples' faces pale with fear. Peter, bold as ever, steps out—actually walking toward Jesus—until doubt swallows his courage. He sinks.

Jesus reaches out, grips his hand, and with a playful smile says:

"Oh, you of little faith, why did you doubt?" (Matthew 14:31).

It's not a scolding. It's a nudge—half-chuckle, half-challenge—the kind of teasing that says, *"I've got you, Peter. Trust Me."* The other disciples, dripping wet and wide-eyed, probably laugh in relief as the storm stills.

This is Jesus the teacher, the friend, the Messiah who used humor to stretch hearts and build trust.

Why Jesus Teased

Good-natured teasing isn't about shame—it's about love. It's the friend who ribs you for forgetting the punchline to your own joke, or the parent who chuckles when you panic over a small mess. Teasing builds bridges, eases tension, and invites growth.

Jesus knew this. His playful quips weren't random; they were discipleship with a grin. His teasing:

- Strengthened bonds, turning a ragtag group into family.

- Eased fears, reminding disciples He was always near.

- Sparked growth, nudging them beyond

their doubts.

- Made truth unforgettable—because a well-timed quip lingers forever.

"Oh, You of Little Faith"

Not once, but often, Jesus teased His disciples with this line.

After feeding thousands with a handful of loaves, they sat in a boat, worried about not having bread. Jesus raised an eyebrow: *"You of little faith, why are you discussing that you have no bread?"* (Matthew 16:8). Imagine Him smiling, as if to say: *"You just watched Me feed a crowd. Still worried about lunch?"*

The disciples probably blushed, then laughed, realizing the truth: Jesus is enough.

The "Sons of Thunder"

When Jesus nicknamed James and John "Boanerges"—*Sons of Thunder* (Mark 3:17)—it was affectionate teasing at its finest.

The brothers were fiery. When a Samaritan village rejected Jesus, they wanted to torch it (Luke 9:54). Jesus laughed, shook His head, and the name stuck. Over time, though, thunder softened into love. John, once hotheaded, would one day write, *"God is love"* (1 John 4:8).

Jesus' humor didn't just poke fun. It shaped hearts.

The Emmaus Road

After the resurrection, two disciples trudged toward Emmaus, weighed with grief. Jesus joined them, but they didn't recognize Him.

"What are you discussing?" He asked.

They stared. *"Are you the only one who doesn't know what's happened?"*

Suppressing a grin, He pressed: *"What things?"* (Luke 24:17–19).

It was divine playfulness—a setup that let their hope reignite before He revealed Himself.

When their eyes opened, joy and laughter surely mingled with awe.

"You Feed Them" and "Any Fish?"

When a hungry crowd gathered, Jesus told His disciples: *"You give them something to eat."* (Matthew 14:16). He knew they didn't have enough—but He let them squirm before multiplying food.

Later, after a night of failure at sea, He called from shore: *"Friends, haven't you any fish?"* (John 21:5). He knew their nets were empty. His playful question set the stage for overflowing nets.

It's the kind of grin a teacher gives before revealing the solution—stretching faith with a smile.

Why It Matters

Jesus' teasing wasn't careless. It was intentional, loving, and formative. He used humor to calm storms, shape hearts, and deepen trust.

Imagine Him at your small group today, smiling as He says: *"Still worrying after all I've carried you through?"* Not to shame, but to invite trust. His playfulness reminds us that holiness and laughter walk hand in hand.

Living Jesus' Humor

How can we follow His example?

In parenting: Tease with love. *"No clean socks again? Didn't I show you the laundry room?"*

In friendships: Use humor to lift burdens. *"Still worrying? Didn't God show up last time?"*

In faith-sharing: Tell the stories of Jesus with a grin—let His humor do the work.

Jesus' humor was always kind, never cruel. It built up, never tore down.

Reflection Questions

Faith and Laughter
When has God used a lighthearted moment to ease your fears or strengthen your trust?

Your Nickname

If Jesus gave you a playful nickname to teach and tease, what might it be? How could it spur growth?

Playful Discipleship

How can you use gentle humor this week to encourage someone's faith without belittling them?

Teasing with Love

Think of a time when kind teasing helped you grow. How might Jesus' playful nudges inspire you to trust Him more?

Chapter 3

The Art of Holy Hyperbole

A Marketplace and a Camel

Picture a bustling Jerusalem marketplace at noon. The air is thick with the scent of fresh bread, spices, and sweat. Merchants call out, Roman soldiers clank past, and Pharisees stand with folded arms, their robes spotless, their faces smug.

Jesus steps onto a crate, His voice cutting through the noise:

"You blind guides! You strain out a gnat but swallow a camel!" (Matthew 23:24).

The crowd roars with laughter. A child giggles. A trader smirks. Meanwhile, the Pharisees squirm. Everyone pictures it—a man carefully filtering his wine to avoid a tiny gnat, then gulping down a hump-backed camel.

This wasn't Jesus losing His temper. It was strategic brilliance. His outrageous images—planks jutting from eyes, camels crawling through needles—grabbed attention, sparked laughter, and flipped perspectives. Hyperbole wasn't a throwaway joke. It was a divine wake-up call.

Why Hyperbole Worked

In Jewish culture, exaggeration was an art form. Rabbis often told stories so over-the-top they made listeners laugh before they made them think.

Jesus perfected the form. His hyperbole wasn't random—it was purposeful, designed to:

- Expose hypocrisy with images too absurd to ignore.

- Engage listeners, drawing gasps and chuckles alike.

- Make truth unforgettable—because nobody forgets a camel through a needle's eye.

- Reveal God's heart, showing holiness is about love, not nitpicking rules.

Even His word choices carried punch. In Matthew 7:3–5, *dokos* means a load-bearing beam, not a twig. In Matthew 23:24, *kamelos* is Israel's largest unclean animal. These weren't accidents. They were carefully chosen absurdities—ridiculous enough to make crowds laugh and Pharisees fidget.

The Plank in Your Eye

Imagine a man stumbling through the market, a timber beam jutting from his eye, bumping into stalls as he insists he can perform delicate eye surgery on a friend. The crowd bursts out laughing.

That's Jesus' point in Matthew 7:3–5: we're quick to magnify others' flaws while ignoring our own.

His humor exposed hypocrisy with a smile, not a scowl.

Today He might grin at your family table: *"Frustrated with your sibling's mess? Check that plank of pride first."* His exaggeration doesn't shame. It redirects.

Gnats vs. Camels

Back in the marketplace, Jesus sharpened the joke: Pharisees straining wine to avoid swallowing a tiny gnat, then gulping down a camel—humps and all.

Gnats were the smallest unclean pests; camels the largest unclean animals. The image is cartoonish, hilarious, and unforgettable. The lesson is piercing: they obsessed over minor details while neglecting weightier matters like justice, mercy, and faith.

Today He might smile at your office desk: *"Double-checking every typo but nursing a camel-sized grudge against your coworker?"* His hyperbole makes us laugh, then think.

A Camel Through a Needle's Eye

On a Galilean hillside, a wealthy man asked how to inherit eternal life. The crowd leaned in, dazzled by his riches. Jesus stunned them:

"It's easier for a camel to go through the eye of a needle than for a rich person to enter the kingdom of God." (Matthew 19:24).

The absurdity hit hard. The largest animal squeezing through the tiniest hole? Impossible. The image carried the point: wealth can't buy the kingdom. Only grace can.

Today, He might quip at your bank: *"Think that bonus buys heaven? Try threading a camel through a needle first."*

Chop Off Hands, Pluck Out Eyes

Preaching on a hillside, Jesus said:

"If your right eye causes you to sin, tear it out... better to lose one part of your body than for your whole body to be thrown into hell." (Matthew 5:29–30).

The crowd gasped. Some chuckled nervously. No one thought He meant it literally. The imagery was outrageous by design. It jolted people awake: sin is deadly serious. Holiness matters.

Today He might grin at your phone: *"Better to ditch the screen than let it pull you away from God."* The exaggeration shocks, but it sticks.

Why It Lasted

Years later, the disciples probably laughed together around their own campfires: *"Remember when Jesus said a camel could fit through a needle's eye?"* His hyperbole wasn't side chatter—it was central to His teaching. Laughter glued the truth in their hearts.

Modern research echoes this. Studies show humor improves retention, lowers stress, and deepens connection. Jesus knew this all along. His outrageous images made His lessons unforgettable.

Holiness Meets Hyperbole

Jesus' exaggerations didn't dilute truth. They amplified it. His humor revealed a God who delights in joy, not dry ritual.

Picture Him at your church potluck, smiling as He says: *"Worried about the burnt casserole? Better check for a plank before you judge."*

His hyperbole invites us to laugh at our own flaws, embrace humility, and live with joy. Holiness and humor are not opposites. In Jesus, they belong together.

Reflection Questions

Absurd but True
Which of Jesus' hyperboles—plank, camel, or needle's eye—hits you hardest? Why?

Modern Hyperbole
How could you use a Jesus-style exaggeration to teach a truth to a friend, child, or coworker?

Personal Planks
What "plank" in your life might Jesus highlight

with a grin? How could facing it with joy, not guilt, help you grow?

Craft Your Own

Write a humorous exaggeration for a modern struggle (e.g., materialism, pride). Share it with someone this week.

Chapter 4

Jesus' Parables That Flipped the Script

A Samaritan as the Hero?!

Picture yourself crammed into a Galilean courtyard, the sun beating down, the crowd buzzing with anticipation. Jesus steps forward, His voice warm but sharp, spinning a story about a traveler beaten and left for dead.

A priest passes by. Then a Levite. Holy men who should help. The crowd nods—of course one of them will be the hero.

Then Jesus drops the bombshell:
"But a Samaritan stopped, bandaged the man's wounds, and paid for his care." (Luke 10:25–37)

Gasps ripple. A few nervous chuckles. Jaws drop. The Pharisees scowl.

A Samaritan as the hero? The despised outsider outshining Israel's most respected leaders? Unthinkable. Uncomfortable. Unforgettable.

This wasn't just a nice story—it was satire. A divine curveball that flipped expectations, shattered prejudice, and exposed hearts with a grin.

What Is Satire?

Satire uses humor, irony, or exaggeration to expose folly and reveal truth. Rabbis used it. Prophets used it. Jesus perfected it.

His parables weren't cozy bedtime stories. They were sharp, satirical masterpieces—divine disruptions that mocked pride, challenged prejudice, and spotlighted grace.

Imagine Jesus at your church potluck, telling a story where the overlooked janitor, not the pastor, shows kingdom love. That's the power of His satire—holy, surprising, transformative.

The Good Samaritan: The Hero No One Expected (Luke 10:25–37)

A religious scholar asks smugly, "Who is my neighbor?" expecting a safe answer: *"Your fellow Jews."*

Instead, Jesus paints the picture: a bleeding man ignored by a priest and a Levite—men revered for their holiness. The crowd leans in. Surely a rabbi will save the day.

But Jesus flips the script. A Samaritan—despised as a half-breed heretic—stops, bandages the man's wounds, and pays his bill.

The scholar squirms. The crowd murmurs. Some laugh at the audacity. The punchline lands: the neighbor is the one who showed mercy.

Satire stings. It shatters prejudice and unmasks hypocrisy.

Today, Jesus might tell the story this way: *"A pastor hurries past a homeless man. A worship leader ignores him. But an atheist barista kneels to help."* The twist would shock us into seeing love where we least expect it.

The Pharisee and the Tax Collector: Pride Takes a Fall (Luke 18:9–14)

Two men pray in the temple.

The Pharisee struts, chest puffed: *"God, thank You I'm not like sinners—or that tax collector. I fast. I tithe. I'm righteous!"*

The tax collector can't lift his eyes: *"God, have mercy on me, a sinner."*

The punchline? The tax collector goes home justified. The Pharisee does not.

The crowd gasps. Some chuckle at the irony. The holy man misses God's heart. The traitor finds it.

Imagine Jesus at your Bible study, grinning: *"That guy bragging about his quiet time? The quiet sinner in the back's closer to God."* His satire unmasks pride with a smile.

The Workers in the Vineyard: Unfair Grace (Matthew 20:1–16)

A landowner hires workers at dawn, then at noon, then just before sunset. At day's end, each receives the same wage.

The early workers fume: *"We slaved all day!"*

The landowner shrugs: *"Are you envious because I am generous?"*

Jesus drops the mic: *"The last will be first, and the first will be last."*

The crowd buzzes—some laugh, some squirm. The satire bites. God's grace isn't earned; it's given. And that offends our sense of fairness.

Picture Jesus at your workplace, chuckling: *"Upset your coworker got the same bonus for less work? That's how My grace rolls."*

The Mustard Seed: A Tiny Jab at Pride (Matthew 13:31–32)

Jesus compares God's kingdom to a mustard seed—tiny, scrappy, invasive.

"It grows into a tree where birds perch."

The crowd chuckles. Mustard wasn't a cedar. It was a weed—wild, spreading, unstoppable.

The jab lands: God's kingdom won't look like a polished empire. It'll grow humble, relentless, everywhere.

Today, Jesus might quip at your megachurch: *"Think My kingdom needs a big stage? It's more like a weed breaking through the cracks."*

Why Jesus' Satire Still Hits

Jesus' satire was like an arrow—sharp, precise, tipped with humor. It exposed pride, unraveled prejudice, and reframed grace.

It wasn't entertainment. It was transformation. Holy irony that forced people to laugh, then look in the mirror.

Picture Him at your small group, leaning in with a grin: *"That guy bragging about his giving? Watch him trip over pride before dessert."*

His satire cut deep—but it healed.

Living Jesus' Satire

How do we follow His example?

In conversations: Share a parable with a smile, letting its twist spark curiosity.

In teaching: Use gentle satire to challenge pride (e.g., "Think you're the best at soccer? The one who shares the ball wins God's game.").

In worship: Remember God's kingdom grows in humble, unexpected places, not just grand ones.

Jesus' satire was always kind. Always redemptive. Always pointing toward grace.

Reflection Questions

Flipped Expectations: Which parable (Samaritan, tax collector, vineyard workers, mustard seed) surprises you most? Why?

Grace That Offends: Have you ever wrestled with God's grace feeling "unfair"? How does Jesus' satire reshape that struggle?

Kingdom Perspective: Where in your life might you be overlooking mustard-seed beginnings God intends to grow?

Craft Your Satire: Write a short, Jesus-style parable that flips a modern norm (e.g., materialism, status). Share and discuss it.

Chapter 5

Righteousness with a Razor Edge

Jesus vs. the Experts

Picture a tense showdown in a Galilean synagogue, the air thick with the scent of parchment and incense. Pharisees, their robes crisp and their faces smug, corner Jesus with a trick question about the Sabbath, expecting to trap Him.

Jesus doesn't flinch. Instead, He leans in, a sly grin spreading across His face, and says:
"Have you never read what David did...?" (Mark 2:25).

The crowd buzzes. The disciples smirk. The Pharisees freeze—their own Scripture expertise turned against them. Did the carpenter's son just sass the religious elite? Oh yes—and it was glorious.

This is Jesus at His sharpest, wielding sarcasm like a surgeon's scalpel to cut through pride and reveal truth with a twinkle in His eye.

Sarcasm, Bible-Style

We often think of sarcasm as biting or mean, but in Scripture it's a divine art form. Think of Elijah mocking Baal's prophets: *"Shout louder—maybe your god is napping!"* (1 Kings 18:27).

Jesus carried that tradition forward, using irony to expose folly and redirect hearts. His sarcasm wasn't about tearing down—it was about building up, cutting through pride to clear the way for grace.

Imagine Him at your church debate, grinning as He quips:
"Quoting Scripture to win an argument? Maybe read the part about love first."

His words sting, but they spark transformation.

"Have You Never Read...?" (Mark 2:25)

The Pharisees pounce when Jesus' disciples pluck grain on the Sabbath, accusing them of breaking holy law. Jesus doesn't argue theology. He goes for the jugular with a grin:
"Have you never read what David did when he was hungry?"

The Greek verb *anaginōskō* means not only "to read" but also "to read and understand." The jab lands hard: these Scripture experts, who hand-copied scrolls, missed the point.

David broke ritual rules to meet human need, and God approved. Jesus' sarcasm exposes their obsession with rules over mercy. They're left speechless.

Picture Jesus at your Bible study, chuckling:
"Read the Bible cover to cover, but missed the chapter on kindness?"

His irony doesn't mock—it redirects, pointing to God's priorities.

Gnats, Camels, and Loopholes (Matthew 23:16–24; Mark 7:9–13)

In a crowded Jerusalem square, Jesus lights into the Pharisees' petty legalism. They swear oaths by the temple but dodge them if sworn by its gold. They sidestep family responsibilities by claiming their money is "set apart for God."

He drips irony:
"You have a fine way of rejecting God's commands to keep your traditions!" (Mark 7:9).

Then He drops the killer line:
"You blind guides! You strain out a gnat but swallow a camel!" (Matthew 23:24).

The crowd laughs, picturing a Pharisee filtering wine for a tiny bug while gulping down a massive camel. The absurdity exposes their hypocrisy: nitpicking rituals while ignoring justice.

Today He might smirk at your office:
"Obsessed with perfect emails but dodging the apology you owe? That's a camel-sized blind spot."

"Tell That Fox…" (Luke 13:32)

When word comes that Herod wants Him dead, Jesus doesn't panic. He brushes it off with a quip:

"Go tell that fox, 'I'm casting out demons and healing today and tomorrow, and on the third day I'll finish My course.'"

Calling Herod a "fox" wasn't flattery. In Jewish culture, foxes symbolized weakness and trickery. The jab lands: Herod might look sly, but he's no lion. God's plan is unstoppable.

Imagine Jesus at your town hall, grinning:

"Tell that politician I'm still working—My kingdom's bigger than their schemes."

His wit puts power in perspective.

"If You Were Blind…" (John 9:39–41)

After healing a man born blind, Jesus faces skeptical Pharisees. They claim to see clearly. He flips the script with biting irony:

"If you were blind, you would have no guilt; but since you say, 'We see,' your guilt remains."

The blind man saw the truth. The "seeing" Pharisees were spiritually blind. The crowd catches the twist—some laugh at the irony, others squirm under its sting.

Imagine Jesus at your conference, quipping: *"Think you've got faith all figured out? The rookie in the back might see Me clearer."*

His words cut pride but invite humility.

Why Sarcasm Worked

Jesus' sarcasm was lightning—quick, sharp, unforgettable. It left no room for pride and pointed straight to God's mercy.

His jabs weren't cruel. They were loving, clearing away arrogance so grace could take root. Jewish teachers used irony, but Jesus perfected it, blending wit with divine wisdom. His sarcasm made Pharisees squirm but gave seekers hope, showing a kingdom where humility trumps self-righteousness.

Picture Him at your small group, leaning in with a grin:
"Arguing over theology? Maybe check what love says first."

Not about winning—about redirecting hearts.

Living Jesus' Sarcasm

How can we follow His example? Sarcasm can be tricky—ours often wounds without healing—but Jesus shows us how to use it with love:

- **In conversations**: Use gentle irony to challenge a friend's pride.

- **In teaching**: Share a Gospel quip with a smile, letting Jesus' wit spark curiosity.

- **In self-reflection**: Laugh at your own flaws with Jesus' lens.

Jesus' sarcasm was always kind, always redemptive, always pointing toward grace.

Reflection Questions

Holy Irony: How does seeing Jesus use sarcasm as a teaching tool change your view of Him? What does it reveal about His love?

Blind Spots: The Pharisees "strained gnats but swallowed camels." Where might you be missing God's heart by focusing on small details?

Receiving the Sting: When has someone used sharp but loving words to expose pride in your life? How did it help you grow?

Craft Your Quip: Write a Jesus-style sarcastic quip for a modern issue (e.g., obsession with status). Share it with a friend or group and discuss its impact.

Chapter 6

Would Jesus Make You Laugh?

Picture Jesus at your local coffee shop, the hum of espresso machines mingling with the chatter of morning commuters. You slide into the booth across from Him, heart heavy with a question about faith. You brace for a sermon, but He leans back, a grin spreading across His face, and quips, "Worried about that? Maybe check the plank in your eye first." You laugh, tension melting, and suddenly the truth clicks: God's got this.

This is Jesus—not just the greatest teacher in history, but the most engaging, joy-filled person you could ever meet. His wit, satire, and playful banter weren't side notes—they were a blueprint for how truth and joy belong together, in His day and ours.

Jesus' humor wasn't just for Galilean hillsides or first-century crowds. It's for us—parents juggling chaos, workers facing deadlines, friends sharing faith over coffee. His laughter disarmed doubters, softened hard truths, and built bonds that lasted lifetimes. This chapter is about bringing that laughter into your everyday life, letting Jesus' joy shape how you live, love, and worship.

Humor's Power Then and Now

Jesus used humor like a master artist, painting truth with bold, joyful strokes. His wit served four key purposes:

- **Disarming doubters**, opening hearts with a clever quip or surprising twist.

- **Softening hard truths**, making lessons like humility or grace easier to swallow.

- **Making truth unforgettable**, because images like camels through needles stick forever.

- **Building relationships**, bonding disciples through shared laughter and playful nudges.

Think of the plank-in-the-eye quip (Matthew 7:3–5) or the Samaritan hero (Luke 10:25–37)—these weren't just teachings; they were moments of connection, sparking laughter that glued truth to hearts. Today, that same power still works. A pastor's witty sermon illustration makes you rethink forgiveness. A parent's playful tease helps a child learn honesty. A friend's gentle quip breaks the ice with a skeptic. Jesus knew humor's strength, and He invites us to use it, too.

Joy Is Holiness

We often picture faith as serious—somber prayers, weighty sermons, furrowed brows. But Jesus radiated joy. He turned water to wine at a wedding, laughing with the guests (John 2:1–11). Children flocked to Him, drawn to His warmth (Matthew 19:14). He told His disciples, "My joy may be in you, and… your joy may be complete" (John 15:11). Holiness and happiness weren't opposites for Jesus—they were partners. His laughter wasn't a distraction from faith; it was faith in action, a reflection of a God who "sits in the heavens and laughs" (Psalm 2:4).

This joy extended to worship. Imagine Jesus singing a hymn with His disciples, His smile lighting up the room (Matthew 26:30). His parables and quips weren't just for teaching—they were worship, celebrating God's kingdom with delight. Today, He might join your worship team, chuckling, "Think those off-key notes bother Me? My joy's bigger than that." Jesus' humor shows that worship isn't just solemn—it's vibrant, alive with laughter.

Living Jesus' Humor

So how do we follow the Laughing Messiah in our daily lives? Jesus' humor was kind, purposeful, and grace-filled, and we can mirror it in practical ways:

In parenting: Tease your kid about their messy room like Jesus teased Peter: "No clean socks? Didn't I show you the laundry room last week?" Or even, "Messy room? You hiding a camel in there?" The laughter opens their heart to learn.

In the workplace: Lighten a tense meeting with a gentle quip, like, "Stressing over that deadline? God's handled bigger storms than this." It builds bonds and points to faith.

In sharing faith: Share a Gospel story with a smile, like the camel-through-the-needle quip, to spark curiosity in a skeptic. Humor breaks barriers where lectures fail.

In worship: Let laughter be part of your praise. Chuckle at your own mistakes during a hymn, knowing Jesus smiles with you. Joy is worship, too.

I learned this the hard way. Once, trying to teach my daughter about honesty, I lectured her sternly after she "borrowed" cookies from the jar. She shut down. The next time, I tried

Jesus' approach: "Stealing cookies? You must be training for the cookie heist Olympics!" She giggled, apologized, and opened up. Humor, like Jesus' wit, made the truth stick without shame.

Jesus in Your Everyday

Back at that coffee shop, imagine Jesus leaning across the table, His eyes twinkling: "Think you've got faith all figured out? Keep going—My joy's bigger than your worries." His humor wasn't a footnote; it was part of His holiness, a reflection of a God who delights in His people. He laughed with fishermen, teased tax collectors, and outsmarted Pharisees with a grin. Today, He's laughing with you—through the chaos of parenting, the grind of work, the quiet moments of prayer.

This is the challenge: bring Jesus' humor into your life. Share a parable with a friend, letting its twist spark a laugh. Tease your kids with love, not judgment. Worship with a smile, knowing God delights in your joy. Jesus' laughter isn't just a story from the Gospels—it's a gift for today, inviting you to live faith with a grin.

Reflection Questions

Faith and Fun: When has laughter opened a door to spiritual truth for you? How did it change how you see God?

Joy and Holiness: Do you picture holiness as serious or joyful? How does Jesus' humor challenge or reshape that view?

Following His Example: What's one way you can use gentle humor this week to encourage someone in faith or lighten their load?

Laughter in Worship: How might you bring Jesus' joy into your worship—through a smile, a shared laugh, or a playful prayer?

Epilogue: The Grin That Lingers

Picture a quiet evening on the shores of Galilee after the resurrection. The disciples sit around a fire, bellies full of bread and fish Jesus just provided. The night is still, the stars scattered bright above them. John leans back, smiling at a memory. Peter laughs, shaking his head at his own blunders. And there's Jesus—alive, radiant, chuckling with His friends. Death is defeated, sin undone, and yet the moment is filled not with thunder but with laughter. The Messiah of joy has returned, and His grin lingers long after the fire dies down.

That's the Jesus this book has invited you to rediscover. Not just the man of sorrows, though He bore them fully. Not just the teacher of truth, though He taught with unmatched authority. But the Savior who laughed, teased, and used wit to bind hearts to His own. His humor wasn't a footnote—it was central to His ministry, revealing that God's kingdom is not only holy but happy.

We've walked through His hyperbole, satire, teasing, and sarcasm, seeing how each carried truth with joy. We've imagined Him at our workplaces, our homes, our coffee shops, and our churches. And we've learned that His wit wasn't confined to ancient hillsides—it still speaks, still disarms, still heals today.

So now it's your turn. Bring His joy into your story. Let laughter soften tense moments with your children. Let wit disarm conflict at work. Let playful banter deepen friendships. And when faith feels heavy, remember the grin of Jesus—the one who turned water into wine, welcomed children to His lap, and ribbed Peter when he sank.

Faith is serious, yes. But it is never joyless. Because the God we follow laughs, and His laughter is our strength.

So smile.
Laugh.
Teach with a twinkle.
Worship with a grin.

And live every day knowing that Jesus' joy is not behind you but with you, right now. His humor was holy then, and it's holy still.

One Last Question

Where in your life do you most need to see Jesus' grin today?

About the Author

 Christian A. Dickinson is an author, speaker, and the President & CEO of Learning Engineered Publishing, where he develops faith-based and secular books, including devotionals, children's literature, and educational resources.

With over twenty years as a principal, teacher, and coach, he has shaped the next generation of students and educators—a passion that fuels his writing.

One day, he asked himself: "Was Jesus actually... funny?" That question led him to deep dive into Scripture, history, and early Christian art, where he discovered Jesus wasn't just the greatest teacher of all time. He was also witty, engaging, and unexpectedly funny.

Dickinson's Christian books include *FULL CIR-CLE 360: A Devotional for Athletes* and *Micah 6:8: A Prophetic Bridge to Jesus.* He and his wife, Morgan, co-author Christian character-building children's books, including *Fruits of the Spirit for Kids.*

Beyond faith-based work, he publishes STEM magazines, economic literacy books for class-rooms, and non-faith-based parenting re-sources.

When he's not writing, publishing, or mentor-ing, you can find him debating the best por-trayals of Jesus, brainstorming over coffee, or secretly laughing at his own dad jokes.

He believes that if Jesus were here today, He'd still be teaching through humor, flipping tables—and yes, making His disciples laugh along the way.

More by Christian A. Dickinson

If you enjoyed *Jesus was Funnier Than You Think*, you may also appreciate these Christ-centered resources:

Jesus Was Funnier Than You Think: Unlocking His Wit, Wisdom, and Unexpected Humor

A fresh look at the wit and humor of Jesus Christ — revealing the brilliant, joyful ways He taught truth and disarmed pride.

Every Tear Remembered: God's Presence in Our Grief

A reflection on sorrow, healing, and hope through the lens of God's enduring love.

The Curse of Time: Time Began When Eternity Broke

A theological and personal exploration of time as a consequence of sin—not a neutral part of creation. Drawing from Scripture, Church Fathers, and moments of divine encounter, this book challenges the assumption that time was God's original design and invites readers to rediscover the eternal now of God's presence.

Roar of 'Ēzer: Reclaiming God's Vision for Women's Strength

From Eden's garden to the early church, God named women *'ēzer*—rescuer, strength-bearer, equal partner in His image. This compelling biblical exploration invites women to rise, not as shadows but as co-laborers in God's kingdom. With Scripture, story, and a call to courage, *Roar of 'Ēzer* reveals that women were never meant to shrink. They were always meant to roar.

The Prophetic Equation: Thirty Prophets. One Christ. Zero Coincidence.

An exploration of how thirty prophetic voices across centuries, kingdoms, and crises converge with stunning precision in Jesus Christ —

revealing that Scripture is not random, but a masterpiece of divine design.

Micah 6:8: A Prophetic Bridge to Jesus

A concise biblical commentary exploring how one ancient verse points forward to the life and ministry of Christ.

It's All or Nothing: How Jesus Raised the Standard from Tithing to Full Surrender

A biblical commentary challenging traditional views of tithing by exploring Jesus' call to radical, Spirit-led generosity.

FULL CIRCLE: PREGAME — A Devotional Series for Athletes

Before the whistle blows and the lights come up, PREGAME challenges athletes to prepare their hearts as well as their bodies. With powerful stories, Scripture reflections, and real talk from the locker room, Coach Dickinson and Anthony "Diso" Paradiso equip competitors to lead with faith, play with integrity, and honor Christ in every moment.

Seeing the Humor: A Glossary & Next Steps

Picture Jesus by a crackling campfire, sparks dancing into a starry Galilean sky, His laugh warming the night as He hands you this glossary to decode His wit. These terms, woven through the Gospels, reveal the humor of the Laughing Messiah—use them to spot His joy in every story.

Key Terms

Hyperbole: Wild exaggeration to make truth stick, like picturing a camel squeezing through a needle's eye to show wealth won't buy heaven (Ch. 3).
Try it: tell your kid their messy room could hide a camel!

Satire: Sharp humor exposing folly, like making a Samaritan the hero to flip prejudice on its head (Ch. 4).
Next time you see pride, share a story that gently flips it.

Rabbinic Humor: Playful wordplay Jewish teachers loved, perfected by Jesus' teasing nicknames like "Sons of Thunder" for fiery disciples (Ch. 2).
Try a loving nickname to nudge a friend's faith.

Irony: Saying one thing, meaning another—like asking smug Pharisees, "Have you never read...?" when they'd memorized Scripture (Ch. 5).
Use gentle irony to point a coworker to truth.

Parable: Short stories with surprise twists, like a tax collector outshining a Pharisee, revealing God's grace (Ch. 4).
Share a parable's twist to spark faith in a skeptic.

Messianic Joy: Jesus' ministry overflowed with laughter, not just sacrifice, inviting us to live

with His grin (Epilogue).
Let His joy shine in your next prayer.

Absurdity in Teaching: Outrageous imagery, like a plank in the eye, to make spiritual truths unforgettable (Ch. 3).
Paint a funny picture to teach a lesson this week.

Take It Further: Grab your Bible and circle a Gospel moment where one of these terms shines. Share it with a friend or group, and let Jesus' wit spark a laugh.

Recommended Books for Deeper Study

Keep chasing the Laughing Messiah with these resources, each one a spark to light up Jesus' wit and joy in your faith journey:

The Humor of Christ by Elton Trueblood — A classic unpacking Jesus' witty teachings, perfect for spotting His quips in the Gospels.

Between Heaven and Mirth by James Martin — A fun, accessible guide to joy and humor in faith, ideal for beginners wanting to laugh with Jesus.

The Parables of Jesus by Joachim Jeremias — A deep dive into Jesus' satirical stories, revealing their cultural sting.

Ante Pacem by Graydon E. Snyder — Early Christian art shows a smiling Jesus, reminding us of His joy.

Jesus Laughed by Robert Darden — A lively look at laughter's role in Scripture, perfect for seeing Jesus' warmth in every quip.

The Wit and Wisdom of Jesus by Charles B. Cousar — A study of Jesus' sharp, engaging style, ideal for unpacking His irony.

Jesus the King by Tim Keller — A journey through Mark's Gospel, highlighting Jesus' wisdom and humor.

The Chosen (TV Series) — This modern portrayal of a laughing, teasing Jesus brings the Gospels to life.

Take It Further: Pick one resource this week—read a chapter, watch an episode—and journal how it helps you see Jesus' humor. Share your insights with a friend or group.

Why This Matters

Picture Jesus by that Galilean campfire, the scent of cedar and smoke mingling as He teases His disciples, their laughter echoing under the stars (Ch. 1). His quips about planks in eyes (Ch. 3), sarcastic jabs at Pharisees' pride (Ch. 5), and satirical parables flipping cultural norms (Ch. 4) reveal a Savior who taught with joy.

This isn't just ancient history—it's a blueprint for living faith today. Humor isn't a distraction; it's a divine gift that deepens faith, breaks barriers, and mirrors God's heart, as Scripture ("A cheerful heart is good medicine," Proverbs 17:22) and science (a 2019 study found laughter boosts endorphins by 27%) confirm.

Jesus' laughter invites you to see the Good News with fresh eyes. Imagine Him at your coffee shop, grinning: "Still sweating the small stuff? Try loving like Me—it's funnier." His wit shows that holiness and humor are partners, not opposites.

So grab your Bible, reread a Gospel chapter, and circle a moment of His wit—a plank, a camel, a sassy quip. Share it with a friend, laugh together, and let His joy spark your faith. Live with a smile, knowing the Laughing Messiah walks with you.

Take It Further: This week, share a Gospel story with a humorous twist (e.g., the camel-through-the-needle quip) with someone in your life. Discuss how Jesus' joy changes how you see faith.

Bible Study Resources

Looking to dive deeper?
We've created a **6-week Bible study** to help you explore the themes of this book in a meaningful and interactive way. Whether studying alone or with a group, this guide will provide Scripture, reflection questions, and action steps to apply what you've learned.

Scan the QR code below to access the complete study guide and additional resources.